Going From
Mind Full to *mindful*

This Journal Belongs to:

_____

FOR A LITTLE INSPIRATION
follow along at:

🅞 @JUNEANDLUCY

🅕 @JUNEANDLUCY

WWW. JUNELUCY.COM

✉ **Love free goodies?** Join our newsletter by emailing us at **freebies@junelucy.com** to receive freebies, discounts and sales info. Let us know which book you bought by putting the book title in the subject line of your email.

Shop our other books at
www.junelucy.com

For questions and customer service, email us at
support@junelucy.com

Mindfulness Journal: the basics

We live in a fast-paced society where it often feels like every waking hour is consumed by deadlines, chores, errands, and obligations. When we do get a few quiet moments to ourselves we often spend them scouring social media or tuning in to the 24-hour news cycle. We often forget to take a few peaceful moments to listen to our own voice. Mindfulness is the practice of being intentionally present and focusing inward toward our own body and mind. Mindfulness is achieved through gratitude work, meditation, deep breathing, and learning to be intentionally present in the moment. A few minutes each day focusing on mindfulness can lead to reduced stress, better sleep, and a more equipped toolkit to handle the ups and downs that life throws at you.

HOW TO USE THIS JOURNAL:

Each two-page layout provides space for several mindfulness practices that can easily be accomplished in a few minutes each day. Start by listing three things you are grateful for. They can be as small as a warm mug of your favorite vanilla chai tea, or as big as an anniversary or promotion.

Next, spend a few moments checking in on how you are feeling, both physically and mentally. Are you excited about upcoming plans, anxious about a deadline, or simply content? Does your body feel rested, achy, or energized?

Then take a minute for a Sensory Check. List one thing in the following categories that has brought you joy recently: touch (fuzzy slippers), smell (fresh cut lawn), taste (homemade sourdough bread), sound (the birds you heard singing), and sight (your sleeping cat). This practice takes gratitude down to a basic level and reminds you that there is beauty hidden in every minute of the day.

Make an effort to do a few minutes of deep breathing or meditation every day. There are great apps for guided meditation that will help talk you through the practice or turn on sounds of a babbling brook or rain on a roof. Some find it helpful to repeat a mantra in their head, such as "I breathe in light and I breathe out love."

Finally, spend three to five minutes journaling in a stream-of-consciousness style. Whatever you are feeling, mentally, physically, and spiritually – write it down! This type of freestyle journaling has been shown to encourage a more present and appreciative mind, ease fears and promote a peaceful mindset.

DATE: _____ S M T W T F S

I AM GRATEFUL FOR:

1. _____

2. _____

3. _____

HOW AM I FEELING: TODAY I EXPERIENCED:

_____   TOUCH _____

_____   SMELL _____

_____   TASTE _____

                                     SOUND _____

X X X X X X X X X X X   SIGHT _____

JUST BREATHE

meditation + deep breathing

Meditation/Deep Breathing Exercises: _____ minutes

☐ Guided   ☐ Silent   ☐ Background Noise/Music _____

☐ Mantra _____

☐ No mantra

How I felt before (mark on scale with an "X") and how I felt after (mark on scale with a "O")

Physically 0 _____ 10

Mentally   0 _____ 10

be here now

Take 3-5 minutes to journal whatever is on your mind and heart. Write in a stream-of-consciousness style and let go of all judgment. If you get stuck, simply write down the sounds you hear, the things you see, and the feelings you experience.

DATE: _____ S M T W T F S

I AM GRATEFUL FOR:

1. _____
2. _____
3. _____

sensory check

HOW AM I FEELING:

_____

_____

_____

✗ ✗ ✗ ✗ ✗ ✗ ✗ ✗ ✗ ✗ ✗

TODAY I EXPERIENCED:

TOUCH _____

SMELL _____

TASTE _____

SOUND _____

SIGHT _____

JUST BREATHE

meditation + deep breathing

Meditation/Deep Breathing Exercises: _____ minutes

☐ Guided   ☐ Silent   ☐ Background Noise/Music _____

☐ Mantra _____

☐ No mantra

How I felt before (mark on scale with an "X") and how I felt after (mark on scale with a "O")

Physically 0 _____ 10

Mentally   0 _____ 10

be here now

Take 3-5 minutes to journal whatever is on your mind and heart. Write in a stream-of-consciousness style and let go of all judgment. If you get stuck, simply write down the sounds you hear, the things you see, and the feelings you experience.

DATE: _____ S M T W T F S

I AM GRATEFUL FOR:

1. _____

2. _____

3. _____

sensory check

HOW AM I FEELING:

TODAY I EXPERIENCED:

_____

_____

_____

× × × × × × × × × × ×

TOUCH _____

SMELL _____

TASTE _____

SOUND _____

SIGHT _____

JUST BREATHE

meditation + deep breathing

Meditation/Deep Breathing Exercises: _____ minutes

☐ Guided   ☐ Silent   ☐ Background Noise/Music _____

☐ Mantra _____

☐ No mantra

How I felt before (mark on scale with an "X") and how I felt after (mark on scale with a "O")

Physically   0 _____ 10

Mentally   0 _____ 10

be here now

Take 3-5 minutes to journal whatever is on your mind and heart. Write in a stream-of-consciousness style and let go of all judgment. If you get stuck, simply write down the sounds you hear, the things you see, and the feelings you experience.

DATE: _____ S M T W T F S

I AM GRATEFUL FOR:

1. _____

2. _____

3. _____

sensory check

HOW AM I FEELING:

_____

_____

_____

✗ ✗ ✗ ✗ ✗ ✗ ✗ ✗ ✗ ✗ ✗

TODAY I EXPERIENCED:

TOUCH _____

SMELL _____

TASTE _____

SOUND _____

SIGHT _____

JUST BREATHE
meditation + deep breathing

Meditation/Deep Breathing Exercises: _____ minutes

☐ Guided ☐ Silent ☐ Background Noise/Music _____

☐ Mantra _____

☐ No mantra

How I felt before (mark on scale with an "X") and how I felt after (mark on scale with a "O")

Physically 0 _____ 10

Mentally 0 _____ 10

be here now

Take 3-5 minutes to journal whatever is on your mind and heart. Write in a stream-of-consciousness style and let go of all judgment. If you get stuck, simply write down the sounds you hear, the things you see, and the feelings you experience.

DATE: _____ S M T W T F S

I AM GRATEFUL FOR:

1. _____

2. _____

3. _____

_____

sensory check

HOW AM I FEELING:

_____

_____

_____

X X X X X X X X X X X

TODAY I EXPERIENCED:

TOUCH _____

SMELL _____

TASTE _____

SOUND _____

SIGHT _____

JUST BREATHE

meditation + deep breathing

Meditation/Deep Breathing Exercises: _____ minutes

☐ Guided   ☐ Silent   ☐ Background Noise/Music _____

☐ Mantra _____

☐ No mantra

How I felt before (mark on scale with an "X") and how I felt after (mark on scale with a "O")

Physically   0 _____ 10

Mentally   0 _____ 10

be here now

Take 3-5 minutes to journal whatever is on your mind and heart. Write in a stream-of-consciousness style and let go of all judgment. If you get stuck, simply write down the sounds you hear, the things you see, and the feelings you experience.

Creating beautiful moments begins with paying attention to the little things.

A mindful moment

Try a full body scan by starting at the tippy top of your head and describing how your body feels all the way down to your toes. Where are you holding tension? How does it feel to relax each part of your body one at a time? How does your breath feel as you inhale and exhale?

DATE: _____ S M T W T F S

I AM GRATEFUL FOR:

1. _____

2. _____

3. _____

sensory check

HOW AM I FEELING:

_____

_____

_____

✗ ✗ ✗ ✗ ✗ ✗ ✗ ✗ ✗ ✗ ✗

TODAY I EXPERIENCED:

TOUCH _____

SMELL _____

TASTE _____

SOUND _____

SIGHT _____

JUST BREATHE

meditation + deep breathing

Meditation/Deep Breathing Exercises: _____ minutes

☐ Guided   ☐ Silent   ☐ Background Noise/Music _____

☐ Mantra _____

☐ No mantra

How I felt before (mark on scale with an "X") and how I felt after (mark on scale with a "O")

Physically   0 _____ 10

Mentally   0 _____ 10

be here now

Take 3-5 minutes to journal whatever is on your mind and heart. Write in a stream-of-consciousness style and let go of all judgment. If you get stuck, simply write down the sounds you hear, the things you see, and the feelings you experience.

DATE: _____ S M T W T F S

I AM GRATEFUL FOR:

1. _____

2. _____

3. _____

sensory check

HOW AM I FEELING:

_____

_____

_____

✗ ✗ ✗ ✗ ✗ ✗ ✗ ✗ ✗ ✗ ✗

TODAY I EXPERIENCED:

TOUCH _____

SMELL _____

TASTE _____

SOUND _____

SIGHT _____

JUST BREATHE

meditation + deep breathing

Meditation/Deep Breathing Exercises: _____ minutes

☐ Guided   ☐ Silent   ☐ Background Noise/Music _____

☐ Mantra _____

☐ No mantra

How I felt before (mark on scale with an "X") and how I felt after (mark on scale with a "O")

Physically   0 _____ 10

Mentally   0 _____ 10

be here now

Take 3-5 minutes to journal whatever is on your mind and heart. Write in a stream-of-consciousness style and let go of all judgment. If you get stuck, simply write down the sounds you hear, the things you see, and the feelings you experience.

DATE: _____ S M T W T F S

I AM GRATEFUL FOR:

1. _____

2. _____

3. _____

_____

HOW AM I FEELING:

_____

_____

_____

x x x x x x x x x x X

TODAY I EXPERIENCED:

TOUCH _____

SMELL _____

TASTE _____

SOUND _____

SIGHT _____

JUST BREATHE

meditation + deep breathing

Meditation/Deep Breathing Exercises: _____ minutes

☐ Guided ☐ Silent ☐ Background Noise/Music _____

☐ Mantra _____

☐ No mantra

How I felt before (mark on scale with an "X") and how I felt after (mark on scale with a "O")

Physically 0 _____ 10

Mentally 0 _____ 10

be here now

Take 3-5 minutes to journal whatever is on your mind and heart. Write in a stream-of-consciousness style and let go of all judgment. If you get stuck, simply write down the sounds you hear, the things you see, and the feelings you experience.

DATE: _____ S M T W T F S

I AM GRATEFUL FOR:

1. _____

2. _____

3. _____

sensory check

HOW AM I FEELING:

_____

_____

_____

✗ ✗ ✗ ✗ ✗ ✗ ✗ ✗ ✗ ✗ ✗

TODAY I EXPERIENCED:

TOUCH _____

SMELL _____

TASTE _____

SOUND _____

SIGHT _____

JUST BREATHE

meditation + deep breathing

Meditation/Deep Breathing Exercises: _____ minutes

☐ Guided   ☐ Silent   ☐ Background Noise/Music _____

☐ Mantra _____

☐ No mantra

How I felt before (mark on scale with an "X") and how I felt after (mark on scale with a "O")

Physically   0 _____ 10

Mentally   0 _____ 10

be here now

Take 3-5 minutes to journal whatever is on your mind and heart. Write in a stream-of-consciousness style and let go of all judgment. If you get stuck, simply write down the sounds you hear, the things you see, and the feelings you experience.

DATE: _____ S M T W T F S

I AM GRATEFUL FOR:

1. _____
2. _____
3. _____

_____

sensory check

HOW AM I FEELING:

_____

_____

_____

✗ ✗ ✗ ✗ ✗ ✗ ✗ ✗ ✗ ✗ ✗

TODAY I EXPERIENCED:

TOUCH _____

SMELL _____

TASTE _____

SOUND _____

SIGHT _____

JUST BREATHE

meditation + deep breathing

Meditation/Deep Breathing Exercises: _____ minutes

☐ Guided   ☐ Silent   ☐ Background Noise/Music _____

☐ Mantra _____

☐ No mantra

How I felt before (mark on scale with an "X") and how I felt after (mark on scale with a "O")

Physically   0 _____ 10

Mentally   0 _____ 10

be here now

Take 3-5 minutes to journal whatever is on your mind and heart. Write in a stream-of-consciousness style and let go of all judgment. If you get stuck, simply write down the sounds you hear, the things you see, and the feelings you experience.

We can only control
what is happening in
this moment.

A mindful moment

Brainstorm at least ten different mantras that you might find helpful during meditation or deep breathing exercises. Here are a few examples to start: I am content in this moment. I am worthy and enough just as I am. I am grateful for all I have been given. I am exactly where I need to be. As I silence my thoughts, I am listening to my heart.

DATE: _____ S M T W T F S

I AM GRATEFUL FOR:

1. _____

2. _____

3. _____

sensory check

HOW AM I FEELING:

_____

_____

_____

✗ ✗ ✗ ✗ ✗ ✗ ✗ ✗ ✗ ✗ ✗

TODAY I EXPERIENCED:

TOUCH _____

SMELL _____

TASTE _____

SOUND _____

SIGHT _____

JUST BREATHE

meditation + deep breathing

Meditation/Deep Breathing Exercises: _____ minutes

☐ Guided   ☐ Silent   ☐ Background Noise/Music _____

☐ Mantra _____

☐ No mantra

How I felt before (mark on scale with an "X") and how I felt after (mark on scale with a "O")

Physically   0 _____ 10

Mentally   0 _____ 10

be here now

Take 3-5 minutes to journal whatever is on your mind and heart. Write in a stream-of-consciousness style and let go of all judgment. If you get stuck, simply write down the sounds you hear, the things you see, and the feelings you experience.

DATE: _____ S M T W T F S

I AM GRATEFUL FOR:

1. _____

2. _____

3. _____

_____   *sensory check*

HOW AM I FEELING:

_____

_____

_____

× × × × × × × × × × ×

TODAY I EXPERIENCED:

TOUCH _____

SMELL _____

TASTE _____

SOUND _____

SIGHT _____

JUST BREATHE

meditation + deep breathing

Meditation/Deep Breathing Exercises: _____ minutes

☐ Guided   ☐ Silent   ☐ Background Noise/Music _____

☐ Mantra _____

☐ No mantra

How I felt before (mark on scale with an "X") and how I felt after (mark on scale with a "O")

Physically   0 _____ 10

Mentally   0 _____ 10

be here now

Take 3-5 minutes to journal whatever is on your mind and heart. Write in a stream-of-consciousness style and let go of all judgment. If you get stuck, simply write down the sounds you hear, the things you see, and the feelings you experience.

DATE: _____ S M T W T F S

I AM GRATEFUL FOR:

1. _____

2. _____

3. _____

_____   *sensory check*

HOW AM I FEELING:

_____

_____

_____

✗ ✗ ✗ ✗ ✗ ✗ ✗ ✗ ✗ ✗ ✗

TODAY I EXPERIENCED:

TOUCH _____

SMELL _____

TASTE _____

SOUND _____

SIGHT _____

JUST BREATHE
meditation + deep breathing

Meditation/Deep Breathing Exercises: _____ minutes

☐ Guided   ☐ Silent   ☐ Background Noise/Music _____

☐ Mantra   _____

☐ No mantra

How I felt before (mark on scale with an "X") and how I felt after (mark on scale with a "O")

Physically   0 _____ 10

Mentally   0 _____ 10

be here now

Take 3-5 minutes to journal whatever is on your mind and heart. Write in a stream-of-consciousness style and let go of all judgment. If you get stuck, simply write down the sounds you hear, the things you see, and the feelings you experience.

DATE: _____ S M T W T F S

I AM GRATEFUL FOR:

1. _____

2. _____

3. _____

HOW AM I FEELING:

_____

_____

_____

✗ ✗ ✗ ✗ ✗ ✗ ✗ ✗ ✗ ✗ ✗

TODAY I EXPERIENCED:

TOUCH _____

SMELL _____

TASTE _____

SOUND _____

SIGHT _____

JUST BREATHE

meditation + deep breathing

Meditation/Deep Breathing Exercises: _____ minutes

☐ Guided   ☐ Silent   ☐ Background Noise/Music _____

☐ Mantra _____

☐ No mantra

How I felt before (mark on scale with an "X") and how I felt after (mark on scale with a "O")

Physically   0 _____ 10

Mentally   0 _____ 10

be here now

Take 3-5 minutes to journal whatever is on your mind and heart. Write in a stream-of-consciousness style and let go of all judgment. If you get stuck, simply write down the sounds you hear, the things you see, and the feelings you experience.

DATE: _____ S M T W T F S

I AM GRATEFUL FOR:

1. _____

2. _____

3. _____

sensory check

HOW AM I FEELING: TODAY I EXPERIENCED:

_____   TOUCH _____

_____   SMELL _____

_____   TASTE _____

                                 SOUND _____

✗ ✗ ✗ ✗ ✗ ✗ ✗ ✗ ✗ ✗ ✗   SIGHT _____

JUST BREATHE

meditation + deep breathing

Meditation/Deep Breathing Exercises: _____ minutes

☐ Guided   ☐ Silent   ☐ Background Noise/Music _____

☐ Mantra _____

☐ No mantra

How I felt before (mark on scale with an "X") and how I felt after (mark on scale with a "O")

Physically   0 _____ 10

Mentally   0 _____ 10

be here now

Take 3-5 minutes to journal whatever is on your mind and heart. Write in a stream-of-consciousness style and let go of all judgment. If you get stuck, simply write down the sounds you hear, the things you see, and the feelings you experience.

Don't try to calm the storm. The storm will pass. Focus on calming yourself.

A mindful moment

Go to your pantry and grab a food item with interesting characteristics, such as a kiwi, a few raisins, or a pistachio. Now write down everything about that item as if it were your first time ever seeing one. What does the item look like? Smell like? Taste like? What might you compare it to? This exercise is a great introduction to mindfulness as it draws intense focus to an everyday item that you might normally overlook. Mindfulness is about placing intention and attention to each minute of the day.

DATE: _____ S M T W T F S

I AM GRATEFUL FOR:

1. _____
2. _____
3. _____

sensory check

HOW AM I FEELING:

_____
_____
_____

✗ ✗ ✗ ✗ ✗ ✗ ✗ ✗ ✗ ✗ ✗

TODAY I EXPERIENCED:

TOUCH _____
SMELL _____
TASTE _____
SOUND _____
SIGHT _____

JUST BREATHE

meditation + deep breathing

Meditation/Deep Breathing Exercises: _____ minutes

☐ Guided   ☐ Silent   ☐ Background Noise/Music _____

☐ Mantra _____

☐ No mantra

How I felt before (mark on scale with an "X") and how I felt after (mark on scale with a "O")

Physically   0 _____ 10

Mentally   0 _____ 10

be here now

Take 3-5 minutes to journal whatever is on your mind and heart. Write in a stream-of-consciousness style and let go of all judgment. If you get stuck, simply write down the sounds you hear, the things you see, and the feelings you experience.

DATE: _____ S M T W T F S

I AM GRATEFUL FOR:

1. _____
2. _____
3. _____

sensory check

HOW AM I FEELING:

_____

_____

_____

✗ ✗ ✗ ✗ ✗ ✗ ✗ ✗ ✗ ✗ ✗

TODAY I EXPERIENCED:

TOUCH _____

SMELL _____

TASTE _____

SOUND _____

SIGHT _____

JUST BREATHE

meditation + deep breathing

Meditation/Deep Breathing Exercises: _____ minutes

☐ Guided   ☐ Silent   ☐ Background Noise/Music _____

☐ Mantra _____

☐ No mantra

How I felt before (mark on scale with an "X") and how I felt after (mark on scale with a "O")

Physically   0 _____ 10

Mentally   0 _____ 10

be here now

Take 3-5 minutes to journal whatever is on your mind and heart. Write in a stream-of-consciousness style and let go of all judgment. If you get stuck, simply write down the sounds you hear, the things you see, and the feelings you experience.

DATE: _____ S M T W T F S

I AM GRATEFUL FOR:

1. _____

2. _____

3. _____

sensory check

HOW AM I FEELING:

_____

_____

_____

× × × × × × × × × × ×

TODAY I EXPERIENCED:

TOUCH _____

SMELL _____

TASTE _____

SOUND _____

SIGHT _____

JUST BREATHE

meditation + deep breathing

Meditation/Deep Breathing Exercises: _____ minutes

☐ Guided   ☐ Silent   ☐ Background Noise/Music _____

☐ Mantra _____

☐ No mantra

How I felt before (mark on scale with an "X") and how I felt after (mark on scale with a "O")

Physically   0 _____ 10

Mentally   0 _____ 10

be here now

Take 3-5 minutes to journal whatever is on your mind and heart. Write in a stream-of-consciousness style and let go of all judgment. If you get stuck, simply write down the sounds you hear, the things you see, and the feelings you experience.

DATE: _____ S M T W T F S

I AM GRATEFUL FOR:

1. _____

2. _____

3. _____

_____

sensory check

HOW AM I FEELING:

_____

_____

_____

✗ ✗ ✗ ✗ ✗ ✗ ✗ ✗ ✗ ✗ ✗

TODAY I EXPERIENCED:

TOUCH _____

SMELL _____

TASTE _____

SOUND _____

SIGHT _____

JUST BREATHE

meditation + deep breathing

Meditation/Deep Breathing Exercises: _____ minutes

☐ Guided   ☐ Silent   ☐ Background Noise/Music _____

☐ Mantra _____

☐ No mantra

How I felt before (mark on scale with an "X") and how I felt after (mark on scale with a "O")

Physically   0 _____ 10

Mentally   0 _____ 10

be here now

Take 3-5 minutes to journal whatever is on your mind and heart. Write in a stream-of-consciousness style and let go of all judgment. If you get stuck, simply write down the sounds you hear, the things you see, and the feelings you experience.

DATE: _____ S M T W T F S

I AM GRATEFUL FOR:

1. _____

2. _____

3. _____

sensory check

HOW AM I FEELING:

_____

_____

_____

✗ ✗ ✗ ✗ ✗ ✗ ✗ ✗ ✗ ✗ ✗

TODAY I EXPERIENCED:

TOUCH _____

SMELL _____

TASTE _____

SOUND _____

SIGHT _____

JUST BREATHE

meditation + deep breathing

Meditation/Deep Breathing Exercises: _____ minutes

☐ Guided   ☐ Silent   ☐ Background Noise/Music _____

☐ Mantra _____

☐ No mantra

How I felt before (mark on scale with an "X") and how I felt after (mark on scale with a "O")

Physically   0 _____ 10

Mentally   0 _____ 10

be here now

Take 3-5 minutes to journal whatever is on your mind and heart. Write in a stream-of-consciousness style and let go of all judgment. If you get stuck, simply write down the sounds you hear, the things you see, and the feelings you experience.

Pay attention
to your intention.

A mindful moment

We often eat mindlessly, squeezing in a quick 15-minute meal at our desk or lounging in front of the TV with a bag of potato chips. This promotes a disconnect between ourselves and the food that nourishes us. Pick a meal today to practice mindful eating. Describe how you prepared the food and how it tastes. Write down different tastes, textures, and flavor combinations as you truly sit in the moment with your meal.

DATE: _____ S M T W T F S

I AM GRATEFUL FOR:

1. _____

2. _____

3. _____

_____

sensory check

HOW AM I FEELING:

_____

_____

_____

✗ ✗ ✗ ✗ ✗ ✗ ✗ ✗ ✗ ✗ ✗

TODAY I EXPERIENCED:

TOUCH _____

SMELL _____

TASTE _____

SOUND _____

SIGHT _____

JUST BREATHE
meditation + deep breathing

Meditation/Deep Breathing Exercises: _____ minutes

☐ Guided   ☐ Silent   ☐ Background Noise/Music _____

☐ Mantra _____

☐ No mantra

How I felt before (mark on scale with an "X") and how I felt after (mark on scale with a "O")

Physically   0 _____ 10

Mentally   0 _____ 10

be here now

Take 3-5 minutes to journal whatever is on your mind and heart. Write in a stream-of-consciousness style and let go of all judgment. If you get stuck, simply write down the sounds you hear, the things you see, and the feelings you experience.

DATE: _____ S M T W T F S

I AM GRATEFUL FOR:

1. _____
2. _____
3. _____

_____

HOW AM I FEELING:

_____
_____
_____

✗ ✗ ✗ ✗ ✗ ✗ ✗ ✗ ✗ ✗ ✗

TODAY I EXPERIENCED:

TOUCH _____
SMELL _____
TASTE _____
SOUND _____
SIGHT _____

JUST BREATHE

meditation + deep breathing

Meditation/Deep Breathing Exercises: _____ minutes

☐ Guided   ☐ Silent   ☐ Background Noise/Music _____

☐ Mantra _____

☐ No mantra

How I felt before (mark on scale with an "X") and how I felt after (mark on scale with a "O")

Physically   0 _____ 10

Mentally   0 _____ 10

be here now

Take 3-5 minutes to journal whatever is on your mind and heart. Write in a stream-of-consciousness style and let go of all judgment. If you get stuck, simply write down the sounds you hear, the things you see, and the feelings you experience.

DATE: _____ S M T W T F S

I AM GRATEFUL FOR:

1. _____
2. _____
3. _____

sensory check

HOW AM I FEELING:

_____
_____
_____

✗ ✗ ✗ ✗ ✗ ✗ ✗ ✗ ✗ ✗ ✗

TODAY I EXPERIENCED:

TOUCH _____
SMELL _____
TASTE _____
SOUND _____
SIGHT _____

JUST BREATHE

meditation + deep breathing

Meditation/Deep Breathing Exercises: _____ minutes

☐ Guided   ☐ Silent   ☐ Background Noise/Music _____

☐ Mantra _____

☐ No mantra

How I felt before (mark on scale with an "X") and how I felt after (mark on scale with a "O")

Physically   0 _____ 10

Mentally   0 _____ 10

be here now

Take 3-5 minutes to journal whatever is on your mind and heart. Write in a stream-of-consciousness style and let go of all judgment. If you get stuck, simply write down the sounds you hear, the things you see, and the feelings you experience.

DATE: _____ S M T W T F S

I AM GRATEFUL FOR:

1. _____

2. _____

3. _____

sensory check

HOW AM I FEELING:

_____

_____

_____

✗ ✗ ✗ ✗ ✗ ✗ ✗ ✗ ✗ ✗ ✗

TODAY I EXPERIENCED:

TOUCH _____

SMELL _____

TASTE _____

SOUND _____

SIGHT _____

JUST BREATHE

meditation + deep breathing

Meditation/Deep Breathing Exercises: _____ minutes

☐ Guided   ☐ Silent   ☐ Background Noise/Music _____

☐ Mantra _____

☐ No mantra

How I felt before (mark on scale with an "X") and how I felt after (mark on scale with a "O")

Physically   0 _____ 10

Mentally   0 _____ 10

be here now

Take 3-5 minutes to journal whatever is on your mind and heart. Write in a stream-of-consciousness style and let go of all judgment. If you get stuck, simply write down the sounds you hear, the things you see, and the feelings you experience.

DATE: _____ S M T W T F S

I AM GRATEFUL FOR:

1. _____

2. _____

3. _____

sensory check

HOW AM I FEELING:

_____

_____

_____

✗ ✗ ✗ ✗ ✗ ✗ ✗ ✗ ✗ ✗ ✗

TODAY I EXPERIENCED:

TOUCH _____

SMELL _____

TASTE _____

SOUND _____

SIGHT _____

JUST BREATHE

meditation + deep breathing

Meditation/Deep Breathing Exercises: _____ minutes

☐ Guided   ☐ Silent   ☐ Background Noise/Music _____

☐ Mantra _____

☐ No mantra

How I felt before (mark on scale with an "X") and how I felt after (mark on scale with a "O")

Physically   0 _____ 10

Mentally   0 _____ 10

be here now

Take 3-5 minutes to journal whatever is on your mind and heart. Write in a stream-of-consciousness style and let go of all judgment. If you get stuck, simply write down the sounds you hear, the things you see, and the feelings you experience.

Deep breaths are love notes to your body.

A mindful moment

Go for a walk in an area that you are comfortable and familiar with, such as a nearby park or your neighborhood. Instead of mindlessly retracing the steps you have taken many times, open your eyes to the sights and sounds you don't normally notice. Whether it is a neighbor's silly lawn gnome, how green the grass is, or the sound the trees make as the wind rustles their leaves, come home and write down all of the beauty you experienced that you may normally tune out. This exercise helps teach us grounded presence and the ability to put intention into our day-to-day activities.

DATE: _____ S M T W T F S

I AM GRATEFUL FOR:

1. _____
2. _____
3. _____

sensory check

HOW AM I FEELING:

_____

_____

_____

✗ ✗ ✗ ✗ ✗ ✗ ✗ ✗ ✗ ✗ ✗

TODAY I EXPERIENCED:

TOUCH _____

SMELL _____

TASTE _____

SOUND _____

SIGHT _____

JUST BREATHE

meditation + deep breathing

Meditation/Deep Breathing Exercises: _____ minutes

☐ Guided   ☐ Silent   ☐ Background Noise/Music _____

☐ Mantra _____

☐ No mantra

How I felt before (mark on scale with an "X") and how I felt after (mark on scale with a "O")

Physically   0 _____ 10

Mentally   0 _____ 10

be here now

Take 3-5 minutes to journal whatever is on your mind and heart. Write in a stream-of-consciousness style and let go of all judgment. If you get stuck, simply write down the sounds you hear, the things you see, and the feelings you experience.

DATE: _____ S M T W T F S

I AM GRATEFUL FOR:

1. _____

2. _____

3. _____

HOW AM I FEELING:

TODAY I EXPERIENCED:

_____

_____

_____

✗ ✗ ✗ ✗ ✗ ✗ ✗ ✗ ✗ ✗ ✗

TOUCH _____

SMELL _____

TASTE _____

SOUND _____

SIGHT _____

JUST BREATHE

meditation + deep breathing

Meditation/Deep Breathing Exercises: _____ minutes

☐ Guided ☐ Silent ☐ Background Noise/Music _____

☐ Mantra _____

☐ No mantra

How I felt before (mark on scale with an "X") and how I felt after (mark on scale with a "O")

Physically 0 _____ 10

Mentally 0 _____ 10

be here now

Take 3-5 minutes to journal whatever is on your mind and heart. Write in a stream-of-consciousness style and let go of all judgment. If you get stuck, simply write down the sounds you hear, the things you see, and the feelings you experience.

DATE: _____ S M T W T F S

I AM GRATEFUL FOR:

1. _____
2. _____
3. _____

sensory check

HOW AM I FEELING:

_____

_____

_____

✗ ✗ ✗ ✗ ✗ ✗ ✗ ✗ ✗ ✗ ✗

TODAY I EXPERIENCED:

TOUCH _____

SMELL _____

TASTE _____

SOUND _____

SIGHT _____

JUST BREATHE

meditation + deep breathing

Meditation/Deep Breathing Exercises: _____ minutes

☐ Guided ☐ Silent ☐ Background Noise/Music _____

☐ Mantra _____

☐ No mantra

How I felt before (mark on scale with an "X") and how I felt after (mark on scale with a "O")

Physically 0 _____ 10

Mentally 0 _____ 10

be here now

Take 3-5 minutes to journal whatever is on your mind and heart. Write in a stream-of-consciousness style and let go of all judgment. If you get stuck, simply write down the sounds you hear, the things you see, and the feelings you experience.

DATE: _____ S M T W T F S

I AM GRATEFUL FOR:

1. _____

2. _____

3. _____

_____ *sensory check*

HOW AM I FEELING: TODAY I EXPERIENCED:

_____   TOUCH _____

_____   SMELL _____

_____   TASTE _____

                                     SOUND _____

✗ ✗ ✗ ✗ ✗ ✗ ✗ ✗ ✗ ✗ ✗   SIGHT _____

JUST BREATHE

meditation + deep breathing

Meditation/Deep Breathing Exercises: _____ minutes

☐ Guided   ☐ Silent   ☐ Background Noise/Music _____

☐ Mantra _____

☐ No mantra

How I felt before (mark on scale with an "X") and how I felt after (mark on scale with a "O")

Physically   0 _____ 10

Mentally   0 _____ 10

be here now

Take 3-5 minutes to journal whatever is on your mind and heart. Write in a stream-of-consciousness style and let go of all judgment. If you get stuck, simply write down the sounds you hear, the things you see, and the feelings you experience.

DATE: _____ S M T W T F S

I AM GRATEFUL FOR:

1. _____

2. _____

3. _____

_____

sensory check

HOW AM I FEELING:

_____

_____

_____

✗ ✗ ✗ ✗ ✗ ✗ ✗ ✗ ✗ ✗ ✗

TODAY I EXPERIENCED:

TOUCH _____

SMELL _____

TASTE _____

SOUND _____

SIGHT _____

JUST BREATHE

meditation + deep breathing

Meditation/Deep Breathing Exercises: _____ minutes

☐ Guided   ☐ Silent   ☐ Background Noise/Music _____

☐ Mantra _____

☐ No mantra

How I felt before (mark on scale with an "X") and how I felt after (mark on scale with a "O")

Physically   0 _____ 10

Mentally   0 _____ 10

be here now

Take 3-5 minutes to journal whatever is on your mind and heart. Write in a stream-of-consciousness style and let go of all judgment. If you get stuck, simply write down the sounds you hear, the things you see, and the feelings you experience.

Life is only what is
happening in this
very moment.

A mindful moment

In today's world, we can purchase almost anything with the click of a button. Everything from groceries to luxury items appear at our front door on what feels like a constant basis. It is important to be mindful about the material items we possess and what they mean to us. For this exercise, place an item you have recently purchased in front of you or buy an inexpensive item that brings you joy. The item should be something simple like fresh flowers, a new book, or a colorful pen. First, write down all of the physical characteristics of the item. Detail everything from the shape, color, feel, to the size and smell. Next, describe how this item makes you feel and the ways in which it brings you joy. How do you use this item and why do you appreciate it?

DATE: _____ S M T W T F S

I AM GRATEFUL FOR:

1. _____
2. _____
3. _____

sensory check

HOW AM I FEELING:

_____

_____

_____

✗ ✗ ✗ ✗ ✗ ✗ ✗ ✗ ✗ ✗ ✗

TODAY I EXPERIENCED:

TOUCH _____

SMELL _____

TASTE _____

SOUND _____

SIGHT _____

JUST BREATHE

meditation + deep breathing

Meditation/Deep Breathing Exercises: _____ minutes

☐ Guided   ☐ Silent   ☐ Background Noise/Music _____

☐ Mantra _____

☐ No mantra

How I felt before (mark on scale with an "X") and how I felt after (mark on scale with a "O")

Physically   0 _____ 10

Mentally   0 _____ 10

be here now

Take 3-5 minutes to journal whatever is on your mind and heart. Write in a stream-of-consciousness style and let go of all judgment. If you get stuck, simply write down the sounds you hear, the things you see, and the feelings you experience.

DATE: _____ S M T W T F S

I AM GRATEFUL FOR:

1. _____

2. _____

3. _____

_____

HOW AM I FEELING:

_____

_____

_____

✗ ✗ ✗ ✗ ✗ ✗ ✗ ✗ ✗ ✗ ✗

TODAY I EXPERIENCED:

TOUCH _____

SMELL _____

TASTE _____

SOUND _____

SIGHT _____

JUST BREATHE

meditation + deep breathing

Meditation/Deep Breathing Exercises: _____ minutes

☐ Guided   ☐ Silent   ☐ Background Noise/Music _____

☐ Mantra _____

☐ No mantra

How I felt before (mark on scale with an "X") and how I felt after (mark on scale with a "O")

Physically   0 _____ 10

Mentally   0 _____ 10

be here now

Take 3-5 minutes to journal whatever is on your mind and heart. Write in a stream-of-consciousness style and let go of all judgment. If you get stuck, simply write down the sounds you hear, the things you see, and the feelings you experience.

DATE: _____ S M T W T F S

I AM GRATEFUL FOR:

1. _____
2. _____
3. _____

sensory check

HOW AM I FEELING:

_____
_____
_____

x x x x x x x x x x X

TODAY I EXPERIENCED:

TOUCH _____
SMELL _____
TASTE _____
SOUND _____
SIGHT _____

JUST BREATHE

meditation + deep breathing

Meditation/Deep Breathing Exercises: _____ minutes

☐ Guided   ☐ Silent   ☐ Background Noise/Music _____

☐ Mantra _____

☐ No mantra

How I felt before (mark on scale with an "X") and how I felt after (mark on scale with a "O")

Physically   0 _____ 10

Mentally   0 _____ 10

be here now

Take 3-5 minutes to journal whatever is on your mind and heart. Write in a stream-of-consciousness style and let go of all judgment. If you get stuck, simply write down the sounds you hear, the things you see, and the feelings you experience.

DATE: _____ S M T W T F S

I AM GRATEFUL FOR:

1. _____

2. _____

3. _____

_____

sensory check

HOW AM I FEELING: TODAY I EXPERIENCED:

_____   TOUCH _____

_____   SMELL _____

_____   TASTE _____

                             SOUND _____

X X X X X X X X X X X   SIGHT _____

JUST BREATHE

meditation + deep breathing

Meditation/Deep Breathing Exercises: _____ minutes

☐ Guided   ☐ Silent   ☐ Background Noise/Music _____

☐ Mantra   _____

☐ No mantra

How I felt before (mark on scale with an "X") and how I felt after (mark on scale with a "O")

Physically   0 _____ 10

Mentally   0 _____ 10

be here now

Take 3-5 minutes to journal whatever is on your mind and heart. Write in a stream-of-consciousness style and let go of all judgment. If you get stuck, simply write down the sounds you hear, the things you see, and the feelings you experience.

DATE: _____ S M T W T F S

I AM GRATEFUL FOR:

1. _____
2. _____
3. _____

sensory check

HOW AM I FEELING:

_____

_____

_____

✗ ✗ ✗ ✗ ✗ ✗ ✗ ✗ ✗ ✗ ✗

TODAY I EXPERIENCED:

TOUCH _____

SMELL _____

TASTE _____

SOUND _____

SIGHT _____

JUST BREATHE

meditation + deep breathing

Meditation/Deep Breathing Exercises: _____ minutes

☐ Guided   ☐ Silent   ☐ Background Noise/Music _____

☐ Mantra _____

☐ No mantra

How I felt before (mark on scale with an "X") and how I felt after (mark on scale with a "O")

Physically   0 _____ 10

Mentally   0 _____ 10

be here now

Take 3-5 minutes to journal whatever is on your mind and heart. Write in a stream-of-consciousness style and let go of all judgment. If you get stuck, simply write down the sounds you hear, the things you see, and the feelings you experience.

Mindfulness is the
answer to anxiety.

A mindful moment

Today, choose to do a household chore that you don't normally enjoy or have been putting off. Maybe it's unloading the dishwasher, running to the dry cleaner, or scrubbing your shower tiles. Instead of begrudgingly performing this action, put some intention into it. Write down all the work that goes into that chore and how great you feel once it is accomplished. Thank your body for allowing you to complete the chore and use the time when doing the chore to practice some deep breathwork.

DATE: _____ S M T W T F S

I AM GRATEFUL FOR:

1. _____

2. _____

3. _____

HOW AM I FEELING:

_____

_____

_____

✕ ✕ ✕ ✕ ✕ ✕ ✕ ✕ ✕ ✕ ✕

sensory check

TODAY I EXPERIENCED:

TOUCH _____

SMELL _____

TASTE _____

SOUND _____

SIGHT _____

JUST BREATHE

meditation + deep breathing

Meditation/Deep Breathing Exercises: _____ minutes

☐ Guided   ☐ Silent   ☐ Background Noise/Music _____

☐ Mantra _____

☐ No mantra

How I felt before (mark on scale with an "X") and how I felt after (mark on scale with a "O")

Physically   0 _____ 10

Mentally   0 _____ 10

be here now

Take 3-5 minutes to journal whatever is on your mind and heart. Write in a stream-of-consciousness style and let go of all judgment. If you get stuck, simply write down the sounds you hear, the things you see, and the feelings you experience.

DATE: _____ S M T W T F S

I AM GRATEFUL FOR:

1. _____
2. _____
3. _____

sensory check

HOW AM I FEELING:

_____

_____

_____

✗ ✗ ✗ ✗ ✗ ✗ ✗ ✗ ✗ ✗ ✗

TODAY I EXPERIENCED:

TOUCH _____

SMELL _____

TASTE _____

SOUND _____

SIGHT _____

JUST BREATHE
meditation + deep breathing

Meditation/Deep Breathing Exercises: _____ minutes

☐ Guided   ☐ Silent   ☐ Background Noise/Music _____

☐ Mantra _____

☐ No mantra

How I felt before (mark on scale with an "X") and how I felt after (mark on scale with a "O")

Physically   0 _____ 10

Mentally   0 _____ 10

be here now

Take 3-5 minutes to journal whatever is on your mind and heart. Write in a stream-of-consciousness style and let go of all judgment. If you get stuck, simply write down the sounds you hear, the things you see, and the feelings you experience.

DATE: _____ S M T W T F S

I AM GRATEFUL FOR:

1. _____
2. _____
3. _____

HOW AM I FEELING:

_____
_____
_____

✗ ✗ ✗ ✗ ✗ ✗ ✗ ✗ ✗ ✗ ✗

sensory check

TODAY I EXPERIENCED:

TOUCH _____
SMELL _____
TASTE _____
SOUND _____
SIGHT _____

JUST BREATHE

meditation + deep breathing

Meditation/Deep Breathing Exercises: _____ minutes

☐ Guided   ☐ Silent   ☐ Background Noise/Music _____

☐ Mantra   _____

☐ No mantra

How I felt before (mark on scale with an "X") and how I felt after (mark on scale with a "O")

Physically   0 _____ 10

Mentally   0 _____ 10

be here now

Take 3-5 minutes to journal whatever is on your mind and heart. Write in a stream-of-consciousness style and let go of all judgment. If you get stuck, simply write down the sounds you hear, the things you see, and the feelings you experience.

DATE: _____ S M T W T F S

I AM GRATEFUL FOR:

1. _____

2. _____

3. _____

_____   *sensory check*

HOW AM I FEELING: TODAY I EXPERIENCED:

_____   TOUCH _____

_____   SMELL _____

_____   TASTE _____

                                 SOUND _____

✗ ✗ ✗ ✗ ✗ ✗ ✗ ✗ ✗ ✗ ✗   SIGHT _____

JUST BREATHE

meditation + deep breathing

Meditation/Deep Breathing Exercises: _____ minutes

☐ Guided   ☐ Silent   ☐ Background Noise/Music _____

☐ Mantra   _____

☐ No mantra

How I felt before (mark on scale with an "X") and how I felt after (mark on scale with a "O")

Physically   0 _____ 10

Mentally   0 _____ 10

be here now

Take 3-5 minutes to journal whatever is on your mind and heart. Write in a stream-of-consciousness style and let go of all judgment. If you get stuck, simply write down the sounds you hear, the things you see, and the feelings you experience.

DATE: _____ S M T W T F S

I AM GRATEFUL FOR:

1. _____

2. _____

3. _____

HOW AM I FEELING:

_____

_____

_____

✗ ✗ ✗ ✗ ✗ ✗ ✗ ✗ ✗ ✗ ✗

sensory check

TODAY I EXPERIENCED:

TOUCH _____

SMELL _____

TASTE _____

SOUND _____

SIGHT _____

JUST BREATHE

meditation + deep breathing

Meditation/Deep Breathing Exercises: _____ minutes

☐ Guided ☐ Silent ☐ Background Noise/Music _____

☐ Mantra _____

☐ No mantra

How I felt before (mark on scale with an "X") and how I felt after (mark on scale with a "O")

Physically 0 _____ 10

Mentally 0 _____ 10

be here now

Take 3-5 minutes to journal whatever is on your mind and heart. Write in a stream-of-consciousness style and let go of all judgment. If you get stuck, simply write down the sounds you hear, the things you see, and the feelings you experience.

With every deep breath
I take, I grow calmer.

A mindful moment

As you go throughout your day, take note of at least 25 different things you are grateful for and write them down as you go. Forcing yourself to come up with a list this long will help you focus on all of the little things you have to be grateful for. It can be as small as getting a perfectly ripe avocado, choosing to wear your coziest sweater, or getting a text from a friend or family member.

DATE: _____ S M T W T F S

I AM GRATEFUL FOR:

1. _____

2. _____

3. _____

_____

sensory check

HOW AM I FEELING:

_____

_____

_____

✗ ✗ ✗ ✗ ✗ ✗ ✗ ✗ ✗ ✗ ✗

TODAY I EXPERIENCED:

TOUCH _____

SMELL _____

TASTE _____

SOUND _____

SIGHT _____

JUST BREATHE

meditation + deep breathing

Meditation/Deep Breathing Exercises: _____ minutes

☐ Guided   ☐ Silent   ☐ Background Noise/Music _____

☐ Mantra _____

☐ No mantra

How I felt before (mark on scale with an "X") and how I felt after (mark on scale with a "O")

Physically   0 _____ 10

Mentally   0 _____ 10

be here now

Take 3-5 minutes to journal whatever is on your mind and heart. Write in a stream-of-consciousness style and let go of all judgment. If you get stuck, simply write down the sounds you hear, the things you see, and the feelings you experience.

DATE: _____ S M T W T F S

I AM GRATEFUL FOR:

1. _____

2. _____

3. _____

HOW AM I FEELING:

_____

_____

_____

✗ ✗ ✗ ✗ ✗ ✗ ✗ ✗ ✗ ✗ ✗

sensory check

TODAY I EXPERIENCED:

TOUCH _____

SMELL _____

TASTE _____

SOUND _____

SIGHT _____

JUST BREATHE

meditation + deep breathing

Meditation/Deep Breathing Exercises: _____ minutes

☐ Guided   ☐ Silent   ☐ Background Noise/Music _____

☐ Mantra _____

☐ No mantra

How I felt before (mark on scale with an "X") and how I felt after (mark on scale with a "O")

Physically   0 _____ 10

Mentally   0 _____ 10

be here now

Take 3-5 minutes to journal whatever is on your mind and heart. Write in a stream-of-consciousness style and let go of all judgment. If you get stuck, simply write down the sounds you hear, the things you see, and the feelings you experience.

DATE: _____ S M T W T F S

I AM GRATEFUL FOR:

1. _____

2. _____

3. _____

sensory check

HOW AM I FEELING:

_____

_____

_____

✕ ✕ ✕ ✕ ✕ ✕ ✕ ✕ ✕ ✕ ✕

TODAY I EXPERIENCED:

TOUCH _____

SMELL _____

TASTE _____

SOUND _____

SIGHT _____

JUST BREATHE

meditation + deep breathing

Meditation/Deep Breathing Exercises: _____ minutes

☐ Guided   ☐ Silent   ☐ Background Noise/Music _____

☐ Mantra _____

☐ No mantra

How I felt before (mark on scale with an "X") and how I felt after (mark on scale with a "O")

Physically   0 _____ 10

Mentally   0 _____ 10

be here now

Take 3-5 minutes to journal whatever is on your mind and heart. Write in a stream-of-consciousness style and let go of all judgment. If you get stuck, simply write down the sounds you hear, the things you see, and the feelings you experience.

DATE: _____ S M T W T F S

I AM GRATEFUL FOR:

1. _____

2. _____

3. _____

_____

sensory check

HOW AM I FEELING:

_____

_____

_____

✗ ✗ ✗ ✗ ✗ ✗ ✗ ✗ ✗ ✗ ✗

TODAY I EXPERIENCED:

TOUCH _____

SMELL _____

TASTE _____

SOUND _____

SIGHT _____

JUST BREATHE

meditation + deep breathing

Meditation/Deep Breathing Exercises: _____ minutes

☐ Guided   ☐ Silent   ☐ Background Noise/Music _____

☐ Mantra _____

☐ No mantra

How I felt before (mark on scale with an "X") and how I felt after (mark on scale with a "O")

Physically   0 _____ 10

Mentally   0 _____ 10

be here now

Take 3-5 minutes to journal whatever is on your mind and heart. Write in a stream-of-consciousness style and let go of all judgment. If you get stuck, simply write down the sounds you hear, the things you see, and the feelings you experience.

DATE: _____ S M T W T F S

I AM GRATEFUL FOR:

1. _____

2. _____

3. _____

_____

sensory check

HOW AM I FEELING:

_____

_____

_____

✗ ✗ ✗ ✗ ✗ ✗ ✗ ✗ ✗ ✗ ✗

TODAY I EXPERIENCED:

TOUCH _____

SMELL _____

TASTE _____

SOUND _____

SIGHT _____

JUST BREATHE
meditation + deep breathing

Meditation/Deep Breathing Exercises: _____ minutes

☐ Guided   ☐ Silent   ☐ Background Noise/Music _____

☐ Mantra _____

☐ No mantra

How I felt before (mark on scale with an "X") and how I felt after (mark on scale with a "O")

Physically   0 _____ 10

Mentally   0 _____ 10

be here now

Take 3-5 minutes to journal whatever is on your mind and heart. Write in a stream-of-consciousness style and let go of all judgment. If you get stuck, simply write down the sounds you hear, the things you see, and the feelings you experience.

The body benefits from
motion and the mind
benefits from quiet.

Made in the USA
Monee, IL
11 May 2021

67834421R00066